PAVED WITH

GOOD INTENTION

# PAVED WITH GOOD INTENTIONS

## A DEMON'S ROADMAP TO YOUR SOUL

C. S. LEWIS

*Edited by Patricia S. Klein*

**HarperSanFrancisco**
*A Division of* HarperCollins*Publishers*

*I willingly believe that the damned are, in one sense, successful, rebels to the end; that the doors of hell are locked on the* inside. *I do not mean that the ghosts may not* wish *to come out of hell, in the vague fashion wherein an envious man 'wishes' to be happy: but they certainly do not will even the first preliminary stages of that self-abandonment through which alone the soul can reach any good. They enjoy forever the horrible freedom they have demanded, and are therefore self-enslaved: just as the blessed, forever submitting to obedience, become through all eternity more and more free.*

—C. S. Lewis, *The Problem of Pain*

# INTRODUCTION

It seemed an innocuous discovery, an obscure notebook with highlighted passages surrounded by scribbles in a crabbed hand. On closer inspection its purposes become clear, its intentions less innocent. It belonged once to a fiend named Wormwood and represents his training under his demon uncle Screwtape. The notebook contains bits of correspondence, annotations, remarks, and the occasional cross-reference. It is, in short, a demon's personal field book, full of instructions, techniques, practices, and observations. A working manual of temptation. A handbook of corruption and destruction. A window into a world of distortion and deception.

There is a current bit of wisdom circulating in our culture of addiction: How do you know when an addict is lying? Answer: His lips are moving. Of course, one could find any number of substitutes for "addict": politician, teenager, corporate executive, cable news host, lawyer. We howl in protest, "He lied!" with the same outrage of a New York tourist complaining about a rigged game of three-card monte: "He cheated!" And of course we aren't really surprised. We know that the game is rigged and we know that we're being lied to—unless we've wrapped ourselves too comfortably in denial (another lovely word from the world of addiction!).

So it is apparently with the Devil: he is a liar. If his lips are moving, he is lying. And as becomes apparent in this fiendish little souvenir, he is happy to employ any strategy to separate humans from "the Enemy" (God), be

they direct lies, diversions, half-truths: deceptions all. His goal is to numb, to corrupt, to
erode virtue into vice—any means necessary
to move us slowly, inexorably away from the
Creator and toward the created.

The question becomes, Do we believe he
is lying to us? Do we believe our game is
rigged? Or are we so far gone that we cannot
recognize these deceptions and think we're
just fine, thank you very much. Before you
answer (before you lie to yourself!), permit
yourself a moment or two to review this
demon's notes. Then make up your own
mind.

—*Patricia S. Klein*

## FIELD NOTE

## Our Mission Statement

The only thing that matters is the extent to which you separate the man from the Enemy. It does not matter how small the sins are provided that their cumulative effect is to edge the man away from the Light and out into the Nothing. Murder is no better than cards if cards can do the trick. Indeed the safest road to Hell is the gradual one—the gentle slope, soft underfoot, without sudden turnings, without milestones, without signposts.

# Re: The Church as a Tool

## *Use the Church itself as a weapon against the Human's Christian faith*

One of our great allies at present is the Church itself. Do not misunderstand me. I do not mean the Church as we see her spread out through all time and space and rooted in eternity, terrible as an army with banners. That, I confess, is a spectacle which makes our boldest tempters uneasy. But fortunately it is quite invisible to these humans. All your patient sees is the half-finished, sham Gothic erection on the new building estate. When he goes inside, he sees the local grocer with rather an oily expression on his face bustling up to offer him one shiny little book containing a liturgy which neither of them understands, and one shabby little book containing corrupt texts of a number of religious lyrics, mostly bad, and in very small print. When he gets to his pew and looks round him he sees just that selection of his neighbours whom he has hitherto avoided. You want to lean pretty heavily on those neighbours. Make his mind flit to and fro between an expression like 'the body of Christ' and the actual faces in the next pew. It matters very little, of course, what kind of people that next pew really contains. You may know one of them to be a great warrior on the Enemy's side. No matter. Your patient, thanks to Our Father Below, is a fool. Provided that any of those neighbours sing out of tune, or have boots that squeak, or double chins, or odd clothes, the patient will quite easily believe that their religion must therefore be somehow ridiculous. At his present stage, you see, he has an idea of 'Christians' in his mind which he supposes to be spiritual but which, in fact, is largely pictorial. His mind is full of togas and sandals and armour and bare legs and the mere fact that the other people in church wear modern clothes is a real—though of course an unconscious—difficulty to him. Never let it come to the surface; never let him ask what he expected them to look like. Keep

3

everything hazy in his mind now, and you will have all eternity wherein to amuse yourself by producing in him the peculiar kind of clarity which Hell affords.

## The Strategy of Disappointment

Work hard, then, on the disappointment or anticlimax which is certainly coming to the patient during his first few weeks as a churchman. The Enemy allows this disappointment to occur on the threshold of every human endeavour. It occurs when the boy who has been enchanted in the nursery by *Stories from the Odyssey* buckles down to really learning Greek. It occurs when lovers have got married and begin the real task of learning to live together. In every department of life it marks the transition from dreaming aspiration to laborious doing. The Enemy takes this risk because He has a curious fantasy of making all these disgusting little human vermin into what He calls His 'free' lovers and servants—'sons' is the word He uses, with His inveterate love of degrading the whole spiritual world by unnatural liaisons with the two-legged animals. Desiring their freedom, He therefore refuses to carry them, by their mere affections and habits, to any of the goals which He sets before them: He leaves them to 'do it on their own'. And there lies our opportunity. But also, remember, there lies our danger. If once they get through this initial dryness successfully, they become much less dependent on emotion and therefore much harder to tempt.

## The Strategy of Diversion

Surely you know that if a man can't be cured of churchgoing, the next best thing is to send him all over the neighbourhood looking for the church that 'suits' him until he becomes a taster or connoisseur of churches.

The reasons are obvious. In the first place the parochial organisation should always be attacked, because, being a unity of place and not of likings, it brings people of different classes and

C. S. LEWIS

psychology together in the kind of unity the Enemy desires. The congregational principle, on the other hand, makes each church into a kind of club, and finally, if all goes well, into a coterie or faction. In the second place, the search for a 'suitable' church makes the man a critic where the Enemy wants him to be a pupil. What He wants of the layman in church is an attitude which may, indeed, be critical in the sense of rejecting what is false or unhelpful, but which is wholly uncritical in the sense that it does not appraise—does not waste time in thinking about what it rejects, but lays itself open in uncommenting, humble receptivity to any nourishment that is going. . . . This attitude, especially during sermons, creates the condition (most hostile to our whole policy) in which platitudes can become really audible to a human soul. There is hardly any sermon, or any book, which may not be dangerous to us if it is received in this temper. So pray bestir yourself and send this fool the round of the neighbouring churches as soon as possible.

# Observations on the Human Thinking Process

## *Jargon: a devil's best ally*

Your man has been accustomed, ever since he was a boy, to have a dozen incompatible philosophies dancing about together inside his head. He doesn't think of doctrines as primarily 'true' or 'false', but as 'academic' or 'practical', 'outworn' or 'contemporary', 'conventional' or 'ruthless'. Jargon, not argument, is your best ally in keeping him from the Church. Don't waste time trying to make him think that materialism is *true!* Make him think it is strong, or stark, or courageous—that it is the philosophy of the future. That's the sort of thing he cares about.

## *Fiendish tips on sloppy thinking in Humans*

Thanks to processes which we set at work in them centuries ago, they find it all but impossible to believe in the unfamiliar while the familiar is

7

before their eyes. Keep pressing home on him the *ordinariness* of things. Above all, do not attempt to use science (I mean, the real sciences) as a defence against Christianity. They will positively encourage him to think about realities he can't touch and see. There have been sad cases among the modern physicists. If he must dabble in science, keep him on economics and sociology; don't let him get away from that invaluable 'real life'. But the best of all is to let him read no science but to give him a grand general idea that he knows it all and that everything he happens to have picked up in casual talk and reading is 'the results of modern investigation'. Do remember you are there to fuddle him.

### A great technique for fuddling an 'intellectual'

The Historical Point of View, put briefly, means that when a learned man is presented with any statement in an ancient author, the one question he never asks is whether it is true.

He asks who influenced the ancient writer, and
how far the statement is consistent with what he
said in other books, and what phase in the
writer's development, or in the general history
of thought, it illustrates, and how it affected
later writers, and how often it has been misun-
derstood (specially by the learned man's own
colleagues) and what the general course of
criticism on it has been for the last ten years,
and what is the 'present state of the question'.
To regard the ancient writer as a possible source
of knowledge—to anticipate that what he said
could possibly modify your thoughts or your
behaviour—this would be rejected as unutter-
ably simple-minded. And since we cannot de-
ceive the whole human race all the time, it is
most important thus to cut every generation
off from all others; for where learning makes a
free commerce between the ages there is always
the danger that the characteristic errors of one
may be corrected by the characteristic truths
of another. But thanks be to Our Father and

the Historical Point of View, great scholars are now as little nourished by the past as the most ignorant mechanic who holds that 'history is bunk'.

# How to Corrupt Home Life

*Pointer #1*

Keep his mind on the inner life. He thinks his conversion is something *inside* him and his attention is therefore chiefly turned at present to the states of his own mind—or rather to that very expurgated version of them which is all you should allow him to see. Encourage this. <u>Keep his mind off the most elementary duties by directing it to the most advanced and spiritual ones.</u> Aggravate that most useful human characteristic, the horror and neglect of the obvious. You must bring him to a condition in which he can practise self-examination for an hour without discovering any of those facts about himself which are perfectly clear to anyone who has ever lived in the same house with him or worked in the same office.

C. S. LEWIS

## *Pointer #2*

It is, no doubt, impossible to prevent his praying
for his mother, but we have means of rendering
the prayers innocuous. Make sure that they are
always very 'spiritual', <u>that he is always concerned with the state of her soul and never with
her rheumatism.</u> Two advantages will follow. In
the first place, his attention will be kept on what
he regards as her sins, by which, with a little
guidance from you, he can be induced to mean
any of her actions which are inconvenient or irritating to himself. Thus you can keep rubbing
the wounds of the day a little sorer even while
he is on his knees; the operation is not at all
difficult and you will find it very entertaining.
In the second place, since his ideas about her
soul will be very crude and often erroneous, he
will, in some degree, be praying for an imaginary
person, and it will be your task to make that
imaginary person daily less and less like the real
mother—the sharp-tongued old lady at the
breakfast table. In time, you may get the cleavage

so wide that no thought or feeling from his prayers for the imagined mother will ever flow over into his treatment of the real one. I have had patients of my own so well in hand that they could be turned at a moment's notice from impassioned prayer for a wife's or son's 'soul' to beating or insulting the real wife or son without a qualm.

## Pointer #3

When two humans have lived together for many years it usually happens that each has tones of voice and expressions of face which are almost unendurably irritating to the other. Work on that. <u>Bring fully into the consciousness of your patient that particular lift of his mother's eyebrows which he learned to dislike in the nursery,</u> and let him think how much he dislikes it. Let him assume that she knows how annoying it is and does it to annoy—if you know your job he will not notice the immense improbability of the assumption. And, of course, never let him

13

suspect that he has tones and looks which similarly annoy her. As he cannot see or hear himself, this is easily managed.

## Pointer #4

In civilised life domestic hatred usually expresses itself by saying things which would appear quite harmless on paper (the *words* are not offensive) but in such a voice, or at such a moment, that they are not far short of a blow in the face. To keep this game up you . . . must see to it that each of these two fools has a sort of double standard. <u>Your patient must demand that all his own utterances are to be taken at their face value and judged simply on the actual words, while at the same time judging all his mother's utterances with the fullest and most over-sensitive interpretation of the tone and the context and the suspected intention.</u> She must be encouraged to do the same to him. Hence from every quarrel they can both go away convinced, or very nearly convinced, that they are quite innocent. You know the kind of thing: 'I simply ask her what time dinner will be and she flies into a temper.' Once this habit is well established you have the delightful situation of a human saying things with the express purpose of offending and yet having a grievance when offence is taken.

# The Matter of Prayer

*Squelch Prayer, no matter what!*

The best thing, where it is possible, is to <u>keep the patient from the serious intention of praying altogether.</u> When the patient is an adult recently reconverted to the Enemy's party, like your man, this is best done by encouraging him to remember, or to think he remembers, the parrot-like nature of his prayers in childhood. In reaction against that, he may be persuaded to aim at something entirely spontaneous, inward, informal, and unregularised; and what this will actually mean to a beginner will be an effort to produce in himself a vaguely devotional *mood* in which real concentration of will and intelligence have no part. One of their poets, Coleridge, has recorded that he did not pray 'with moving lips and bended knees' but merely 'composed his spirit to love' and indulged 'a sense of supplication'. That is exactly the sort of prayer we want;

and since it bears a superficial resemblance to the prayer of silence as practised by those who are very far advanced in the Enemy's service, clever and lazy patients can be taken in by it for quite a long time. At the very least, they can be persuaded that the bodily position makes no difference to their prayers; for they constantly forget, what you must always remember, that they are animals and that whatever their bodies do affects their souls. It is funny how mortals always picture us as putting things into their minds: in reality our best work is done by keeping things out.

### The Strategy of Redirection—*away from the Enemy and towards himself and his own feelings*

Whenever they are attending to the Enemy Himself we are defeated, but there are ways of preventing them from doing so. The simplest is to <u>turn their gaze away from Him towards</u>

<u>themselves.</u> Keep them watching their own minds and trying to produce *feelings* there by the action of their own wills. When they meant to ask Him for charity, let them, instead, start trying to manufacture charitable feelings for themselves and not notice that this is what they are doing. When they meant to pray for courage, let them really be trying to feel brave. When they say they are praying for forgiveness, let them be trying to feel forgiven. Teach them to estimate the value of each prayer by their success in producing the desired feeling; and never let them suspect how much success or failure of that kind depends on whether they are well or ill, fresh or tired, at the moment.

But of course the Enemy will not meantime be idle. Whenever there is prayer, there is danger of His own immediate action. He is cynically indifferent to the dignity of His position, and ours, as pure spirits, and to human animals on their knees He pours out self-knowledge in a quite shameless fashion.

## *Keep the Human praying to an imagined 'God', not to the real Person*

The humans do not start from that direct perception of Him which we, unhappily, cannot avoid. They have never known that ghastly luminosity, that stabbing and searing glare which makes the background of permanent pain to our lives. If you look into your patient's mind when he is praying, you will not find *that*. If you examine the object to which he is attending, you will find that it is a composite object containing many quite ridiculous ingredients. There will be images derived from pictures of the Enemy as He appeared during the discreditable episode known as the Incarnation: there will be vaguer—perhaps quite savage and puerile— images associated with the other two Persons. There will even be some of his own reverence (and of bodily sensations accompanying it) objectified and attributed to the object revered. I have known cases where what the patient called his 'God' was actually *located*—up and to the left at the corner of the bedroom ceiling, or inside his own head, or in a crucifix on the wall. But whatever the nature of the composite object, you must <u>keep him praying to *it*—to the thing that he has made, not to the Person who has made him.</u>

### Danger: the real nakedness of the Human soul in prayer

<u>If ever he consciously directs his prayers 'Not to what I think thou art but to what thou knowest thyself to be', our situation is, for the moment, desperate.</u> Once all his thoughts and images have been flung aside or, if retained, retained with a full recognition of their merely subjective nature, and the man trusts himself to the completely real, external, invisible Presence, there with him in the room and never knowable by him as he is known by it—why, then it is that the incalculable may occur. In avoiding this situation—this real nakedness of the soul in

prayer—you will be helped by the fact that the humans themselves do not desire it as much as they suppose. There's such a thing as getting more than they bargained for!

## The Strategy of Distraction

The use of his 'love' to distract his mind from the Enemy is, of course, obvious, but you reveal what poor use you are making of it when you say that the whole question of distraction and the wandering mind has now become one of the chief subjects of his prayers. That means you have largely failed. When this, or any other distraction, crosses his mind you ought to encourage him to thrust it away by sheer will power and to try to continue the normal prayer as if nothing had happened; once he accepts the distraction as his present problem and lays *that* before the Enemy and makes it the main theme of his prayers and his endeavours, then, so far from doing good, you have done harm. <u>Anything,</u>

even a sin, which has the total effect of moving him close up to the Enemy makes against us in the long run.

## 911: What to do when the Human prays despite your best efforts

Since your patient has contracted the terrible habit of obedience, he will probably continue such 'crude' prayers whatever you do. But you can worry him with the haunting suspicion that the practice is absurd and can have no objective result. Don't forget to use the 'heads I win, tails you lose' argument. If the thing he prays for doesn't happen, then that is one more proof that petitionary prayers don't work; if it does happen, he will, of course, be able to see some of the physical causes which led up to it, and 'therefore it would have happened anyway', and thus a granted prayer becomes just as good a proof as a denied one that prayers are ineffective.

You, being a spirit, will find it difficult to understand how he gets into this confusion. But you must remember that he takes Time for an ultimate reality. He supposes that the Enemy, like himself, sees some things as present, remembers others as past, and anticipates others as future; or even if he believes that the Enemy does not see things that way, yet, in his heart of hearts, he regards this as a peculiarity of the Enemy's mode of perception—he doesn't really think (though he would say he did) that things as the Enemy sees them are things as they are!

C. S. LEWIS

## FIELD NOTE

## War—entertaining but problematic

I must warn you not to hope too much from a
war. Of course a war is entertaining. The
immediate fear and suffering of the humans is a
legitimate and pleasing refreshment for our myr-
iads of toiling workers. But what permanent
good does it do us unless we make use of it for
bringing souls to Our Father Below? . . . Let us
therefore think rather how to use, than how to
enjoy, this European war. For it has certain tendencies inherent in it which are, in themselves,
by no means in our favour. We may hope for a
good deal of cruelty and unchastity. But, if we
are not careful, we shall see thousands turning
in this tribulation to the Enemy, while tens of
thousands who do not go so far as that will
nevertheless have their attention diverted from
themselves to values and causes which they believe to be higher than the self. . . . Consider too

what undesirable deaths occur in wartime. Men are killed in places where they knew they might be killed and to which they go, if they are at all of the Enemy's party, prepared. How much better for us if *all* humans died in costly nursing homes amid doctors who lie, nurses who lie, friends who lie, as we have trained them, promising life to the dying, encouraging the belief that sickness excuses every indulgence, and even, if our workers know their job, withholding all suggestion of a priest lest it should betray to the sick man his true condition! And how disastrous for us is the continual remembrance of death which war enforces. One of our best weapons, contented worldliness, is rendered useless. <u>In wartime not even a human can believe that he is going to live forever.</u>

# Using Emotions

## *Keep the Human worried*

We want him to be in the maximum uncertainty, so that his mind will be filled with contradictory pictures of the future, every one of which arouses hope or fear. <u>There is nothing like suspense and anxiety for barricading a human's mind against the Enemy.</u> He wants men to be concerned with what they do; our business is to keep them thinking about what will happen to them.

## *A Demon's Goal: real hate and fantasy love*

Do what you will, there is going to be some benevolence, as well as some malice, in your patient's soul. The great thing is to <u>direct the malice to his immediate neighbours whom he meets every day and to thrust his benevolence out to the remote circumference, to people he</u>

<u>does not know.</u> The malice thus becomes
wholly real and the benevolence largely imaginary. There is no good at all in inflaming his
hatred of Germans if, at the same time, a perni-
cious habit of charity is growing up between
him and his mother, his employer, and the man
he meets in the train. Think of your man as a
series of concentric circles, his will being the in-
nermost, his intellect coming next, and finally
his fantasy. You can hardly hope, at once, to exclude from all the circles everything that smells
of the Enemy: but you must keep on shoving all
the virtues outward till they are finally located in
the circle of fantasy, and all the desirable quali-
ties inward into the Will. It is only in so far as
they reach the Will and are there embodied in
habits that the virtues are really fatal to us.

**FIELD NOTE**

## Do I show my fiendish face?

I wonder you should ask me whether it is essential to keep the patient in ignorance of your own existence. . . . Our policy, for the moment, is to conceal ourselves. Of course this has not always been so. We are really faced with a cruel dilemma. When the humans disbelieve in our existence we lose all the pleasing results of direct terrorism and we make no magicians. On the other hand, when they believe in us, we cannot make them materialists and sceptics. At least, not yet. I have great hopes that we shall learn in due time how to emotionalise and mythologise their science to such an extent that what is, in effect, a belief in us (though not under that name) will creep in while the human mind remains closed to belief in the Enemy. The 'Life Force', the worship of sex, and some aspects of Psychoanalysis may here prove useful.

If once we can produce our perfect work—the Materialist Magician, the man, not using, but veritably worshipping, what he vaguely calls 'Forces' while denying the existence of 'spirits'—then the end of the war will be in sight. But in the meantime we must obey our orders. I do not think you will have much difficulty in keeping the patient in the dark. The fact that 'devils' are predominantly *comic* figures in the modern imagination will help you. <u>If any faint suspicion of your existence begins to arise in his mind, suggest to him a picture of something in red tights, and persuade him that since he cannot believe in that (it is an old textbook method of confusing them) he therefore cannot believe in you.</u>

# Using Political or Social Stances

## *The Strategy of Extremes*

All extremes, except extreme devotion to the Enemy, are to be encouraged. Not always, of course, but at this period. Some ages are lukewarm and complacent, and then it is our business to soothe them yet faster asleep. Other ages, of which the present is one, are unbalanced and prone to faction, and it is our business to inflame them. Any small coterie, bound together by some interest which other men dislike or ignore, tends to develop inside itself a hothouse mutual admiration, and towards the outer world, a great deal of pride and hatred which is entertained without shame because the 'Cause' is its sponsor and it is thought to be impersonal. Even when the little group exists originally for the Enemy's own purposes, this remains true. We want the Church to be small not only that fewer men may know the Enemy but also that those who do may acquire the uneasy intensity and the defensive self-righteousness of a secret society or a clique. The Church herself is, of course, heavily defended and we have never yet quite succeeded in giving her *all* the characteristics of a faction; but subordinate factions within her have often produced admirable results, from the parties of Paul and of Apollos at Corinth down to the High and Low parties in the Church of England.

## Instructions on moving the Human's faith from primary position to supporting role

Whichever [position towards war] he adopts, your main task will be the same. Let him begin by treating the Patriotism or the Pacifism as a part of his religion. Then let him, under the influence of partisan spirit, come to regard it as the most important part. Then quietly and gradually nurse him on to the stage at which the religion becomes merely part of the 'cause', in which Christianity is valued chiefly because of the excellent arguments it can produce in favour

31

of the British war-effort or of Pacifism. The attitude which you want to guard against is that in which temporal affairs are treated primarily as material for obedience. <u>Once you have made the World an end, and faith a means, you have almost won your man, and it makes very little difference what kind of worldly end he is pursuing.</u> Provided that meetings, pamphlets, policies, movements, causes, and crusades matter more to him than prayers and sacraments and charity, he is ours—and the more 'religious' (on those terms) the more securely ours. I could show you a pretty cageful down here.

## FIELD NOTE

## Noise

Music and silence—how I detest them both! How thankful we should be that ever since Our Father entered Hell—though longer ago than humans, reckoning in light years, could express—<u>no square inch of infernal space and no moment of infernal time has been surrendered to either of those abominable forces, but all has been occupied by Noise</u>—Noise, the grand dynamism, the audible expression of all that is exultant, ruthless, and virile—Noise which alone defends us from silly qualms, despairing scruples and impossible desires. We will make the whole universe a noise in the end. We have already made great strides in this direction as regards the Earth. The melodies and silences of Heaven will be shouted down in the end. But I admit we are not yet loud enough, or anything like it.

C. S. LEWIS

# Re: Peaks and Troughs

*Enemy Intelligence: The Law of Undulation*

Humans are amphibians—half spirit and half animal. . . . As spirits they belong to the eternal world, but as animals they inhabit time. This means that while their spirit can be directed to an eternal object, their bodies, passions, and imaginations are in continual change, for to be in time means to change. <u>Their nearest approach to constancy, therefore, is undulation—the repeated return to a level from which they repeatedly fall back, a series of troughs and peaks.</u> If you had watched your patient carefully you would have seen this undulation in every department of his life—his interest in his work, his affection for his friends, his physical appetites, all go up and down. As long as he lives on earth periods of emotional and bodily richness and liveliness will alternate with periods of numbness and poverty. The dryness and dullness through which your patient is now going are not, as you

34

fondly suppose, your workmanship; they are merely a natural phenomenon which will do us no good unless you make a good use of it.

## Enemy Intelligence: His Goals vs. Our Goals

<u>To us a human is primarily food; our aim is the absorption of its will into ours,</u> the increase of our own area of selfhood at its expense. But the obedience which the Enemy demands of men is quite a different thing. One must face the fact that all the talk about His love for men, and His service being perfect freedom, is not (as one would gladly believe) mere propaganda, but an appalling truth. <u>He really *does* want to fill the universe with a lot of loathsome little replicas of Himself</u>—creatures whose life, on its miniature scale, will be qualitatively like His own, not because He has absorbed them but because their wills freely conform to His. We want cattle who can finally become food; He wants servants who can finally become sons. We want to suck in, He wants to give out. We are empty and would

be filled; He is full and flows over. Our war aim is a world in which Our Father Below has drawn all other beings into himself: the Enemy wants a world full of beings united to Him but still distinct.

## How the Enemy utilizes the earthly phenomenon of peaks and troughs

You must have often wondered why the Enemy does not make more use of His power to be sensibly present to human souls in any degree He chooses and at any moment. But you now see that the Irresistible and the Indisputable are the two weapons which the very nature of His scheme forbids Him to use. Merely to override a human will (as His felt presence in any but the faintest and most mitigated degree would certainly do) would be for Him useless. He cannot ravish. He can only woo. For His ignoble idea is to eat the cake and have it; the creatures are to be one with Him, but yet themselves; merely to cancel them, or assimilate them, will not serve.

He is prepared to do a little overriding at the beginning. He will set them off with communications of His presence which, though faint, seem great to them, with emotional sweetness, and easy conquest over temptation. But He never allows this state of affairs to last long. Sooner or later He withdraws, if not in fact, at least from their conscious experience, all those supports and incentives. He leaves the creature to stand up on its own legs—to carry out from the will alone duties which have lost all relish. It is during such trough periods, much more than during the peak periods, that it is growing into the sort of creature He wants it to be. Hence the prayers offered in the state of dryness are those which please Him best. We can drag our patients along by continual tempting, because we design them only for the table, and the more their will is interfered with the better. He cannot 'tempt' to virtue as we do to vice. He wants them to learn to walk and must therefore take away His hand; and if only the will to walk is really there He is pleased even with their stumbles. Do not be deceived, Wormwood. Our cause is never more in danger than when a human, no longer desiring, but still intending, to do our Enemy's will, looks round upon a universe from which every trace of Him seems to have vanished, and asks why he has been forsaken, and still obeys.

## The Strategy of Exploitation: using the troughs

As always, the first step is to keep knowledge out of his mind. Do not let him suspect the law of undulation. Let him assume that the first ardours of his conversion might have been expected to last, and ought to have lasted, forever, and that his present dryness is an equally permanent condition. Having once got this misconception well fixed in his head, you may then proceed in various ways. It all depends on whether your man is of the desponding type who can be tempted to despair, or of the wishful-thinking type who can be assured that all is well.

The former type is getting rare among the humans. If your patient should happen to belong to it, everything is easy. You have only got to keep him out of the way of experienced Christians (an easy task now-adays), to direct his attention to the appropriate passages in scripture, and then to set him to work on the desperate design of recovering his old feelings by sheer will-power, and the game is ours. If he is of the more hopeful type your job is to make him acquiesce in the present low temperature of his spirit and gradually become content with it, persuading himself that it is not so low after all. In a week or two you will be making him doubt whether the first days of his Christianity were not, perhaps, a little excessive. Talk to him about 'moderation in all things'. <u>If you can once get him to the point of thinking that 'religion is all very well up to a point', you can feel quite happy about his soul.</u> A moderated religion is as good for us as no religion at all—and more amusing.

C. S. LEWIS

# Re: Pleasure

## *Enemy Intelligence: Pleasure*

He's a hedonist at heart. All those fasts and
vigils and stakes and crosses are only a façade.
Or only like foam on the seashore. Out at sea,
out in His sea, there is pleasure, and more pleasure. He makes no secret of it; at His right hand
are 'pleasures for evermore'. Ugh! I don't think
He has the least inkling of that high and austere
mystery to which we rise in the Miserific Vision.
He's vulgar, Wormwood. He has a bourgeois
mind. He has filled His world full of pleasures.
There are things for humans to do all day long
without His minding in the least—sleeping,
washing, eating, drinking, making love, playing,
praying, working. Everything has to be *twisted*
before it's any use to us. We fight under cruel
disadvantages. Nothing is naturally on our side.

## How to use pleasure for our purposes

I know we have won many a soul through pleasure. All the same, it is His invention, not ours. He made the pleasures: all our research so far has not enabled us to produce one. <u>All we can do is to encourage the humans to take the pleasures which our Enemy has produced, at times, or in ways, or in degrees, which He has forbidden.</u> Hence we always try to work away from the natural condition of any pleasure to that in which it is least natural, least redolent of its Maker, and least pleasurable. An ever increasing craving for an ever diminishing pleasure is the formula. It is more certain; and it's better *style*. To get the man's soul and give him *nothing* in return—that is what really gladdens Our Father's heart.

## Don't allow real pleasure! Ever!

And now for your blunders. On your own showing you first of all allowed the patient to read a book he really enjoyed, because he enjoyed it and not in order to make clever remarks about it to his new friends. In the second place, you allowed him to walk down to the old mill and have tea there—a walk through country he really likes, and taken alone. In other words you allowed him two real positive Pleasures. Were you so ignorant as not to see the danger of this? The characteristic of Pains and Pleasures is that they are unmistakably real, and therefore, as far as they go, give the man who feels them a touchstone of reality. Thus if you had been trying to damn your man by the Romantic method . . . you would try to protect him at all costs from any real pain; because, of course, five minutes' genuine toothache would reveal the romantic sorrows for the nonsense they were and unmask your whole stratagem. But you were trying to damn your patient by the World, that is by palming off vanity, bustle, irony, and expensive tedium as pleasures. How can you have failed to see that a *real* pleasure was the last thing you ought to have let him meet? Didn't

you foresee that it would just kill by contrast all
the trumpery which you have been so labori-
ously teaching him to value? And that the sort of
pleasure which the book and the walk gave him
was the most dangerous of all? That it would
peel off from his sensibility the kind of crust
you have been forming on it, and make him feel
that he was coming home, recovering himself?
As a preliminary to detaching him from the
Enemy, you wanted to detach him from himself,
and had made some progress in doing so. Now,
all that is undone.

### Root out the Human's personal pleasures— except of course for the real sins

The deepest likings and impulses of any man
are the raw material, the starting-point, with
which the Enemy has furnished him. To get
him away from those is therefore always a point
gained; even in things indifferent it is always desirable to substitute the standards of the World,
or convention, or fashion, for a human's own

real likings and dislikings. <u>I myself would carry this very far. I would make it a rule to eradicate from my patient any strong personal taste which is not actually a sin,</u> even if it is something quite trivial such as a fondness for county cricket or collecting stamps or drinking cocoa. Such things, I grant you, have nothing of virtue in them; but there is a sort of innocence and humility and self-forgetfulness about them which I distrust. The man who truly and disinterestedly enjoys any one thing in the world, for its own sake, and without caring two-pence what other people say about it, is by that very fact fore-armed against some of our subtlest modes of attack. <u>You should always try to make the patient abandon the people or food or books he really likes in favour of the 'best' people, the 'right' food, the 'important' books.</u> I have known a human defended from strong temptations to social ambition by a still stronger taste for tripe and onions.

**FIELD NOTE**

## On the subject of fun, jokes, flippancy

Fun is closely related to Joy—a sort of emotional froth arising from the play instinct. It is very little use to us. It can sometimes be used, of course, to divert humans from something else which the Enemy would like them to be feeling or doing: but in itself it has wholly undesirable tendencies; it promotes charity, courage, contentment, and many other evils. . . .

The real use of <u>Jokes</u> or Humour is in quite a different direction, and . . . is invaluable as a means of destroying shame. If a man simply lets others pay for him, he is 'mean'; if he boasts of it in a jocular manner and twits his fellows with having been scored off, he is no longer 'mean' but a comical fellow. Mere cowardice is shameful; cowardice boasted of with humorous exaggerations and grotesque gestures can be passed off as funny. Cruelty is shameful—unless the cruel man can represent it as a practical joke. A thousand bawdy, or even blasphemous, jokes do not help towards a man's damnation so much as his discovery that almost anything he wants to do can be done, not only without the disapproval but with the admiration of his fellows, if only it can get itself treated as a Joke. . . .

But flippancy is the best of all. In the first place it is very economical. Only a clever human can make a real Joke about virtue, or indeed about anything else; any of them can be trained to talk *as if* virtue were funny. Among flippant people the Joke is always assumed to have been made. No one actually makes it; but every serious subject is discussed in a manner which implies that they have already found a ridiculous side to it. If prolonged, the habit of Flippancy builds up around a man the finest armour-plating against the Enemy that I know, and it is quite free from the dangers inherent in the other sources of laughter. It is a thousand miles away from joy: it deadens, instead of sharpening, the intellect; and it excites no affection between those who practise it.

# **The Gradual Descent**

## *Obscure the Human's awareness of any and all movement away from the Enemy*

Obviously you are making excellent progress. My only fear is lest in attempting to hurry the patient you awaken him to a sense of his real position. For you and I, who see that position as it really is, must never forget how totally differ-ent it ought to appear to him. <u>We know that we have introduced a change of direction in his course which is already carrying him out of his orbit around the Enemy; but he must be made to imagine that all the choices which have ef-fected this change of course are trivial and revo-cable.</u> He must not be allowed to suspect that he is now, however slowly, heading right away from the sun on a line which will carry him into the cold and dark of utmost space.

For this reason I am almost glad to hear that he is still a churchgoer and a communicant. I know there are dangers in this; but anything is better than that he should realise the break he has made with the first months of his Christian life. As long as he retains externally the habits of a Christian he can still be made to think of himself as one who has adopted a few new friends and amusements but whose spiritual state is much the same as it was six weeks ago. And while he thinks that, <u>we do not have to contend with the explicit repentance of a definite, fully recognised, sin, but only with his vague, though uneasy, feeling that he hasn't been doing very well lately.</u>

## Cautiously manage the Human's vague feelings of spiritual discomfort

This dim uneasiness needs careful handling. If it gets too strong it may wake him up and spoil the whole game. On the other hand, if you suppress it entirely—which, by the by, the Enemy will probably not allow you to do—we lose an element in the situation which can be turned to good account. If such a feeling is allowed to live, but not allowed to become irresistible and flower into real repentance, it has one invaluable tendency. It increases the patient's reluctance to think about the Enemy. All humans at nearly all times have some such reluctance; but when thinking of Him involves facing and intensifying a whole vague cloud of half-conscious guilt, this reluctance is increased tenfold. They hate every idea that suggests Him, just as men in financial embarrassment hate the very sight of a pass-book.

# Corrupting Virtue: Humility

### *How to easily destroy humility*

Your patient has become humble; have you drawn his attention to the fact? All virtues are less formidable to us once the man is aware that he has them, but this is specially true of humility. Catch him at the moment when he is really poor in spirit and smuggle into his mind the gratifying reflection, 'By jove! I'm being humble', and almost immediately pride—pride at his own humility—will appear. If he awakes to the danger and tries to smother this new form of pride, make him proud of his attempt—and so on, through as many stages as you please. But don't try this too long, for fear you awake his sense of humour and proportion, in which case he will merely laugh at you and go to bed.

## The Strategy of Distortion

<u>Conceal from the patient the true end of Humility. Let him think of it not as self-forgetfulness but as a certain kind of opinion (namely, a low opinion) of his own talents and character.</u> Some talents, I gather, he really has. Fix in his mind the idea that humility consists in trying to believe those talents to be less valuable than he believes them to be. No doubt they *are* in fact less valuable than he believes, but that is not the point. The great thing is to make him value an opinion for some quality other than truth, thus introducing an element of dishonesty and make-believe into the heart of what otherwise threatens to become a virtue. By this method thousands of humans have been brought to think that humility means pretty women trying to believe they are ugly and clever men trying to believe they are fools. And since what they are trying to believe may, in some cases, be manifest nonsense, they cannot succeed in believing it and we have the chance of keeping their minds

endlessly revolving on themselves in an effort to achieve the impossible.

## Enemy Intelligence: Humility

To anticipate the Enemy's strategy, we must consider His aims. The Enemy wants to bring the man to a state of mind in which he could design the best cathedral in the world, and know it to be the best, and rejoice in the fact, without being any more (or less) or otherwise glad at having done it than he would be if it had been done by another. The Enemy wants him, in the end, to be so free from any bias in his own favour that he can rejoice in his own talents as frankly and gratefully as in his neighbour's talents—or in a sunrise, an elephant, or a water-fall. He wants each man, in the long run, to be able to recognise all creatures (even himself) as glorious and excellent things. He wants to kill their animal self-love as soon as possible; but it is His long-term policy, I fear, to restore to them a new kind of self-love—a charity and gratitude for all selves, including their own; when they have really learned to love their neighbours as themselves, they will be allowed to love themselves as their neighbours. For we must never forget what is the most repellent and inexplicable trait in our Enemy; He *really* loves the hairless bipeds He has created and always gives back to them with His right hand what He has taken away with His left.

### The Enemy's goal: Humility.
### Our goal: Self-Delusion.

His whole effort . . . will be to get the man's mind off the subject of his own value altogether. He would rather the man thought himself a great architect or a great poet and then forgot about it, than that he should spend much time and pains trying to think himself a bad one. Your efforts to instil either vainglory or false modesty into the patient will therefore be met from the Enemy's side with the obvious reminder that a man is not usually called upon to have an opinion of his own talents at all, since he can very well go on improving them to the best of his ability without deciding on his own precise niche in the temple of Fame. You must try to exclude this reminder from the patient's consciousness at all costs. The Enemy will also try to render real in the patient's mind a doctrine which they all profess but find it difficult to bring home to their feelings—the doctrine that they did not create themselves, that their talents were given them, and that they might as well be proud of the colour of their hair. But always and by all methods the Enemy's aim will be to get the patient's mind off such questions, and yours will be to fix it on them. Even of his sins the Enemy does not want him to think too much: once they are repented, the sooner the man turns his attention outward, the better the Enemy is pleased.

# Gluttony Revisited

### *New spin on an old vice*

The contemptuous way in which you spoke
of gluttony as a means of catching souls . . .
only shows your ignorance. One of the great
achievements of the last hundred years has been
to deaden the human conscience on that subject,
so that by now you will hardly find a sermon
preached or a conscience troubled about it in the
whole length and breadth of Europe. This has
largely been effected by <u>concentrating all our
efforts on gluttony of Delicacy, not gluttony of
Excess.</u> Your patient's mother . . . is a good example. She would be astonished—one day, I
hope, *will* be—to learn that her whole life is enslaved to this kind of sensuality, which is quite
concealed from her by the fact that the quantities
involved are small. But what do quantities matter, provided we can use a human belly and
palate to produce querulousness, impatience, un-
charitableness, and self-concern? . . . She is a

positive terror to hostesses and servants. She is always turning from what has been offered her to say with a demure little sigh and a smile 'Oh please, please . . . *all* I want is a cup of tea, weak but not too weak, and the teeniest weeniest bit of really crisp toast.' You see? Because what she wants is smaller and less costly than what has been set before her, she never recognises as gluttony her determination to get what she wants, however troublesome it may be to others. At the very moment of indulging her appetite she believes that she is practising temperance. In a crowded restaurant she gives a little scream at the plate which some overworked waitress has set before her and says, 'Oh, that's far, far too much! Take it away and bring me about a quarter of it.' If challenged, she would say she was doing this to avoid waste; in reality she does it because the particular shade of delicacy to which we have enslaved her is offended by the sight of more food than she happens to want. The real value of the quiet, unobtrusive work . . . on this old woman can be gauged by the way in which her belly now dominates her whole life.

## Use vanity to enhance gluttony

Now your patient is his mother's son. While working your hardest, quite rightly, on other fronts, you must not neglect a little quiet infiltration in respect of gluttony. Being a male, he is not so likely to be caught by the *'All* I want' camouflage. Males are best turned into gluttons with the help of their vanity. They ought to be made to think themselves very knowing about food, to pique themselves on having found the only restaurant in the town where steaks are really 'properly' cooked. What begins as vanity can then be gradually turned into habit. But, however you approach it, the great thing is to bring him into the state in which the denial of any one indulgence—it matters not which, champagne or tea, *sole colbert* or cigarettes—'puts him out', for then his charity, justice, and obedience are all at your mercy. <u>Mere excess in food is much less valuable than delicacy.</u>

# The Strategy of Corruption: Human Sexuality

*How to distort the ideas of love and marriage*

The Enemy's demand on humans takes the form of a dilemma; *either* complete abstinence *or* unmitigated monogamy. Ever since our Father's first great victory, we have rendered the former very difficult to them. The latter, for the last few centuries, we have been closing up as a way of escape. We have done this through the poets and novelists by persuading the humans that a curious, and usually shortlived, experience which they call 'being in love' is the only respectable ground for marriage; that marriage can, and ought to, render this excitement permanent; and that a marriage which does not do so is no longer binding. This idea is our parody of an idea that came from the Enemy. . . .

The Enemy described a married couple as 'one flesh'. He did not say 'a happily married

<u>couple' or 'a couple who married because they
were in love', but you can make the humans
ignore that.</u> You can also make them forget that
the man they call Paul did not confine it to *married* couples. Mere copulation, for him, make
'one flesh'. You can thus get the humans to ac-
cept as rhetorical eulogies of 'being in love'
what were in fact plain descriptions of the real
significance of sexual intercourse. The truth is
that wherever a man lies with a woman, there,
whether they like it or not, a transcendental
relation is set up between them which must be
eternally enjoyed or eternally endured. From
the true statement that this transcendental relation was intended to produce, and, if obedi-
ently entered into, too often *will* produce,
affection and the family, humans can be made
to infer the false belief that the blend of affection, fear, and desire which they call 'being in
love' is the only thing that makes marriage either happy or holy. . . . In other words, the <u>hu-
mans are to be encouraged to regard as the basis</u>

for marriage a highly-coloured and distorted version of something the Enemy really promises as its result.

## The Strategy of Sexual Misdirection

It is the business of these great masters [deeper down in the Lowerarchy] to produce in every age a general misdirection of what may be called sexual 'taste'. This they do by working through the small circle of popular artists, dressmakers, actresses and advertisers who determine the fashionable type. The aim is to guide each sex away from those members of the other with whom spiritually helpful, happy, and fertile marriages are most likely. Thus we have now for many centuries triumphed over nature to the extent of making certain secondary characteristics of the male (such as the beard) disagreeable to nearly all the females—and there is more in that than you might suppose. As regards the male taste we have varied a good deal. At one time we have directed it to the statuesque and

aristocratic type of beauty, mixing men's vanity
with their desires and encouraging the race to
breed chiefly from the most arrogant and prodi-
gal women. At another, we have selected an ex-
aggeratedly feminine type, faint and languishing,
so that folly and cowardice, and all the general
falseness and littleness of mind which go with
them, shall be at a premium. At present we are
on the opposite tack. The age of jazz has succeeded the age of the waltz, and we now teach
men to like women whose bodies are scarcely
distinguishable from those of boys. Since this is
a kind of beauty even more transitory than most,
we thus aggravate the female's chronic horror
of growing old (with many excellent results)
and render her less willing and less able to bear
children. And that is not all. We have engineered
a great increase in the licence which society allows to the representation of the apparent nude
(not the real nude) in art, and its exhibition on
the stage or the bathing beach. It is all a fake, of
course; the figures in the popular art are falsely
drawn; the real women in bathing suits or tights

are actually pinched in and propped up to make them appear firmer and more slender and more boyish than nature allows a full-grown woman to be. Yet at the same time, the modern world is taught to believe that it is being 'frank' and 'healthy' and getting back to nature. As a result <u>we are more and more directing the desires of men to something which does not exist— making the role of the eye in sexuality more and more important and at the same time making its demands more and more impossible.</u> What follows you can easily forecast!

**FIELD NOTE**

## Exploit raw material

You complain that my last letter does not make it clear whether I regard *being in love* as a desirable state for a human or not. But really, Wormwood, that is the sort of question one expects *them* to ask! Leave them to discuss whether 'Love', or patriotism, or celibacy, or candles on altars, or teetotalism, or education, are 'good' or 'bad'. Can't you see there's no answer? Nothing matters at all except the tendency of a given state of mind, in given circumstances, to move a particular patient at a particular moment nearer to the Enemy or nearer to us. . . . Get it quite clear in your own mind that this state of *falling in love* is not, in itself, necessarily favourable either to us or to the other side. It is simply an occasion which we and the Enemy are both trying to exploit. Like most of the other things which humans are excited about, such as health and sickness, age and youth, or war and peace, it is, from the point of view of the spiritual life, mainly raw material.

63

C. S. LEWIS

# Illusions of Time

## *Enemy Intelligence: On Time and Eternity*

The humans live in time but our Enemy destines
them to eternity. He therefore, I believe, wants
them to attend chiefly to two things, to eternity
itself, and to that point of time which they call
the Present. For the Present is the point at which
time touches eternity. Of the present moment,
and of it only, humans have an experience analo-
gous to the experience which our Enemy has of
reality as a whole; in it alone freedom and actual-
ity are offered them. He would therefore have
them continually concerned either with eternity
(which means being concerned with Him) or
with the Present—either meditating on their
eternal union with, or separation from, Himself,
or else obeying the present voice of conscience,
bearing the present cross, receiving the present
grace, giving thanks for the present pleasure. <u>Our
business is to get them away from the eternal,
and from the Present.</u>

## Keep the focus on the future

We sometimes tempt a human (say a widow or a scholar) to live in the Past. But this is of limited value, for they have some real knowledge of the past and it has a determinate nature and, to that extent, resembles eternity. It is far better to make them live in the Future. Biological necessity makes all their passions point in that direction already, so that thought about the Future inflames hope and fear. Also, it is unknown to them, so that in making them think about it we make them think of unrealities. In a word, the Future is, of all things, the thing *least like* eternity. It is the most completely temporal part of time—for the Past is frozen and no longer flows, and the Present is all lit up with eternal rays. Hence the encouragement we have given to all those schemes of thought such as Creative Evolution, Scientific Humanism, or Communism, which fix men's affections on the Future, on the very core of temporality. Hence nearly all vices are rooted in the future. Gratitude looks to the past and love to the present; fear, avarice, lust, and ambition look ahead. . . .

To be sure, the Enemy wants men to think of the Future too—just so much as is necessary for *now* planning the acts of justice or charity which will probably be their duty tomorrow. The duty of planning the morrow's work is *today's* duty; though its material is borrowed from the future, the duty, like all duties, is in the Present. This is now straw splitting. He does not want men to give the Future their hearts, to place their treasure in it. We do. His ideal is a man who, having worked all day for the good of posterity (if that is his vocation), washes his mind of the whole subject, commits the issue to Heaven, and returns at once to the patience or gratitude demanded by the moment that is passing over him. But we want a man hag-ridden by the Future—haunted by visions of an imminent heaven or hell upon earth—ready to break the Enemy's commands in the present if by so doing we make him think he can attain the one or avert the other—dependent for his faith on the suc-

cess or failure of schemes whose end he will
not live to see. We want a whole race perpetu-
ally in pursuit of the rainbow's end, never honest, nor kind, nor happy *now,* but always using
as mere fuel wherewith to heap the altar of the
future every real gift which is offered them in
the Present.

## Entitlement: a central hoax

<u>Men are not angered by mere misfortune but
by misfortune conceived as injury.</u> And the sense
of injury depends on the feeling that a legitimate claim has been denied. The more claims
on life, therefore, that your patient can be induced to make, the more often he will feel in-
jured and, as a result, ill-tempered. Now you
will have noticed that nothing throws him into a
passion so easily as to find a tract of time which
he reckoned on having at his own disposal un-
expectedly taken from him. It is the unexpected
visitor (when he looked forward to a quiet
evening), or the friend's talkative wife (turning

up when he looked forward to a *tête-à-tête* with
the friend), that throw him out of gear. Now he
is not yet so uncharitable or slothful that these
small demands on his courtesy are *in themselves*
too much for it. They anger him because he regards his time as his own and feels that it is being
stolen.

## The Strategy of Deception, or 'My time is my own'

Zealously guard in his mind the curious assumption 'My time is my own'. Let him have the
feeling that he starts each day as the lawful pos-
sessor of twenty-four hours. Let him feel as a
grievous tax that portion of this property which
he has to make over to his employers, and as a
generous donation that further portion which
he allows to religious duties. But what he must
never be permitted to doubt is that the total
from which these deductions have been made
was, in some mysterious sense, his own personal
birthright.

You have here a delicate task. The assumption which you want him to go on making is so absurd that, if once it is questioned, even we cannot find a shred of argument in its defence. The man can neither make, nor retain, one moment of time; it all comes to him by pure gift; he might as well regard the sun and moon as his chattels. He is also, in theory, committed to a total service of the Enemy; and if the Enemy appeared to him in bodily form and demanded that total service for even one day, he would not refuse. He would be greatly relieved if that one day involved nothing harder than listening to the conversation of a foolish woman; and he would be relieved almost to the pitch of disappointment if for one half-hour in that day the Enemy said 'Now you may go and amuse yourself'. Now if he thinks about his assumption for a moment, even he is bound to realise that he is actually in this situation every day. When I speak of preserving this assumption in his mind, therefore, the last thing I mean you to do is to furnish him with arguments in its defence. There aren't any. Your task is purely negative. Don't let his thoughts come anywhere near it. Wrap a darkness about it, and in the centre of that darkness let his sense of ownership-in-Time lie silent, uninspected, and operative.

**FIELD NOTE**

## Get the Human to treat Christianity as a means—a means to anything!

About the general connection between Christianity and politics, our position is more delicate. Certainly we do not want men to allow their Christianity to flow over into their political life, for the establishment of anything like a really just society would be a major disaster. On the other hand <u>we do want, and want very much, to make men treat Christianity as a means; preferably, of course, as a means to their own advancement, but, failing that, as a means to anything</u>—even to social justice. The thing to do is to get a man at first to value social justice as a thing which the Enemy demands, and then work him on to the stage at which he values Christianity because it may produce social justice. For the Enemy will not be used as a convenience. Men or nations who think they can revive the Faith in order to make a good society might just as well think they can use the stairs of Heaven as a short cut to the nearest chemist's shop. Fortunately it is quite easy to coax humans round this little corner. Only today I have found a passage in a Christian writer where he recommends his own version of Christianity on the ground that 'only such a faith can outlast the death of old cultures and the birth of new civilisations'. <u>You see the little rift? 'Believe this, not because it is true, but for some other reason.' That's the game.</u>

# The Horror of the Same Old Thing

## *Enemy Intelligence: Change*

The horror of the Same Old Thing is one of the most valuable passions we have produced in the human heart—an endless source of heresies in religion, folly in counsel, infidelity in marriage, and inconstancy in friendship. <u>The humans live in time, and experience reality successively. To experience much of it, therefore, they must experience many different things; in other words, they must experience change. And since they need change, the Enemy (being a hedonist at heart) has made change pleasurable to them, just as He has made eating pleasurable. But since He does not wish them to make change, any more than eating, an end in itself, He has balanced the love of change in them by a love of permanence.</u> He has contrived to gratify both tastes together in the very world He has made, by that union of change and permanence which we call Rhythm. He gives them the seasons, each season different yet every year the same, so that spring is always felt as a novelty yet always as the recurrence of an immemorial theme. He gives them in His Church a spiritual year; they change from a fast to a feast, but it is the same feast as before.

## The Strategy of Novelty & Fashion

Just as we pick out and exaggerate the pleasure of eating to produce gluttony, so we pick out this natural pleasantness of change and twist it into a demand for absolute novelty. This demand is entirely our workmanship. If we neglect our duty, men will be not only contented but transported by the mixed novelty and familiarity of snowdrops *this* January, sunrise *this* morning, plum pudding *this* Christmas. Children, until we have taught them better, will be perfectly happy with a seasonal round of games in which conkers succeed hopscotch as regularly as autumn follows summer. Only by our incessant efforts is the demand for infinite, or unrhythmical, change kept up.

This demand is valuable in various ways. In the first place <u>it diminishes pleasure while increasing desire.</u> The pleasure of novelty is by its very nature more subject than any other to the law of diminishing returns. And continued novelty costs money, so that the desire for it spells avarice or unhappiness or both. And again, the more rapacious this desire, the sooner it must eat up all the innocent sources of pleasure and pass on to those the Enemy forbids. Thus by inflaming the horror of the Same Old Thing we have recently made the Arts, for example, less dangerous to us than, perhaps, they have ever been, 'low-brow' and 'high-brow' artists alike being now daily drawn into fresh, and still fresh, excesses of lasciviousness, unreason, cruelty, and pride. Finally, the desire for novelty is indispensable if we are to produce Fashions or Vogues.

<u>The use of Fashions in thought is to distract the attention of men from their real dangers.</u> We direct the fashionable outcry of each generation against those vices of which it is least in

danger and fix its approval on the virtue nearest to that vice which we are trying to make endemic. The game is to have them all running about with fire extinguishers whenever there is a flood, and all crowding to that side of the boat which is already nearly gunwale under. Thus we make it fashionable to expose the dangers of enthusiasm at the very moment when they are all really becoming worldly and lukewarm; a century later, when we are really making them all Byronic and drunk with emotion, the fashionable outcry is directed against the dangers of the mere 'understanding'. Cruel ages are put on their guard against Sentimentality, feckless and idle ones against Respectability, lecherous ones against Puritanism; and whenever all men are really hastening to be slaves or tyrants we make Liberalism the prime bogey.

## The Strategy of Flummery

The greatest triumph of all is to elevate this horror of the Same Old Thing into a philosophy so that nonsense in the intellect may reinforce corruption in the will. . . . The Enemy loves platitudes. Of a proposed course of action He wants men, so far as I can see, to ask very simple questions; is it righteous? is it prudent? is it possible? Now if we can keep men asking 'Is it in accordance with the general movement of our time? Is it progressive or reactionary? Is this the way that History is going?' they will neglect the relevant questions. And the questions they *do* ask are, of course, unanswerable; for they do not know the future, and what the future will be depends very largely on just those choices which they now invoke the future to help them to make. As a result, while their minds are buzzing in this vacuum, we have the better chance to slip in and bend them to the action *we* have decided on. And great work has already been done. Once they knew that some changes were for the better, and others for the worse, and others again indifferent. We have largely removed this knowledge. For the descriptive adjective 'unchanged' we have substituted the emotional adjective 'stagnant'. We have trained them to think of the Future as a promised land which favoured heroes attain—not as something which everyone reaches at the rate of sixty minutes an hour, whatever he does, whoever he is.

# Re: Aging and Death

*Note to Self: Keep the Human alive—it improves our chances of success*

The Enemy has guarded him from you through the first great wave of temptations. But, if only he can be kept alive, you have time itself for your ally. The long, dull, monotonous years of middle-aged prosperity or middle-aged adversity are excellent campaigning weather. You see, it is so hard for these creatures to *persevere*. The routine of adversity, the gradual decay of youthful loves and youthful hopes, the quiet despair (hardly felt as pain) of ever overcoming the chronic temptations with which we have again and again defeated them, the drabness which we create in their lives and the inarticulate resentment with which we teach them to respond to it—all this provides admirable opportunities of wearing out a soul by attrition. If, on the other hand, the middle years prove prosperous, our position is even stronger. <u>Prosperity knits a man</u>

to the World. He feels that he is 'finding his place in it', while really it is finding its place in him. His increasing reputation, his widening circle of acquaintances, his sense of importance, the growing pressure of absorbing and agreeable work, build up in him a sense of being really at home in earth, which is just what we want. You will notice that the young are generally less unwilling to die than the middle-aged and the old.

## *Observations about Human attachments to Heaven and to earth*

The truth is that the Enemy, having oddly destined these mere animals to life in His own eternal world, has guarded them pretty effectively from the danger of feeling at home anywhere else. That is why we must often wish long life to our patients; seventy years is not a day too much for the difficult task of unravelling their souls from Heaven and building up a firm attachment to the earth. While they are young we find them always shooting off at a tangent. Even if we contrive to keep them ignorant of explicit religion, the incalculable winds of fantasy and music and poetry—the mere face of a girl, the song of a bird, or the sight of a horizon—are always blowing our whole structure away. They *will* not apply themselves steadily to worldly advancement, prudent connections, and the policy of safety first. So inveterate is their appetite for Heaven that our best method, at this stage, of attaching them to earth is to make them believe that earth can be turned into Heaven at some future date by politics or eugenics or 'science' or psychology, or what not.

## FIELD NOTE

## Nuancing Spiritual Pride

You must teach him to mistake this contrast between the circle that delights and the circle that bores him for the contrast between Christians and unbelievers. He must be made to feel (he'd better not put it into words) 'how different we Christians are'; and by 'we Christians' he must really, but unknowingly, mean 'my set'; and by 'my set' he must mean not 'The people who, in their charity and humility, have accepted me', but 'The people with whom I associate by right'.

Success here depends on confusing him. If you try to make him explicitly and professedly proud of being a Christian, you will probably fail; the Enemy's warnings are too well known. If, on the other hand, you let the idea of 'we Christians' drop out altogether and merely make him complacent about 'his set', you will produce not true spiritual pride but mere social vanity which, by comparison, is a trumpery, puny little sin. What you want is to keep a sly self-congratulation mixing with all his thoughts and never allow him to raise the question 'What, precisely, am I congratulating myself *about?'* The idea of belonging to an inner ring, of being in a secret, is very sweet to him. Play on that nerve. Teach him . . . to adopt an air of *amusement* at the things the unbelievers say. Some theories which he may meet in modern Christian circles may here prove helpful; theories, I mean, that place the hope of society in some inner ring of 'clerks', some trained minority of theocrats. It is no affair of yours whether those theories are true or false; the great thing is to make Christianity a mystery religion in which he feels himself one of the initiates.

# Those Lovely Vices: Hatred and Cowardice

## Hatred 101

Hatred we can manage. The tension of human nerves during noise, danger, and fatigue makes them prone to any violent emotion and it is only a question of guiding this susceptibility into the right channels. If conscience resists, muddle him. Let him say that he feels hatred not on his own behalf but on that of the women and children, and that a Christian is told to forgive his own, not other people's enemies. In other words <u>let him consider himself sufficiently identified with the women and children to feel hatred on their behalf, but *not* sufficiently identified to regard their enemies as his own and therefore proper objects of forgiveness.</u>

But <u>hatred is best combined with Fear.</u> Cowardice, alone of all the vices, is purely painful—horrible to anticipate, horrible to feel, horrible to remember; Hatred has its pleasures. It is therefore often the *compensation* by which a frightened man reimburses himself for the miseries of Fear. The more he fears, the more he will hate. And Hatred is also a great anodyne for shame. To make a deep wound in his charity, you should therefore first defeat his courage.

## Observations: Never underestimate the courage/cowardice issue

We have made men proud of most vices, but not of cowardice. Whenever we have almost succeeded in doing so, the Enemy permits a war or an earthquake or some other calamity, and at once courage becomes so obviously lovely and important even in human eyes that all our work is undone, and there is still at least one vice of which they feel genuine shame. <u>The danger of inducing cowardice in our patients, therefore, is lest we produce real self-knowledge and self-loathing with consequent</u>

<u>repentance and humility.</u> And in fact, in the last war, thousands of humans, by discovering their own cowardice, discovered the whole moral world for the first time. In peace we can make many of them ignore good and evil entirely; in danger, the issue is forced upon them in a guise to which even we cannot blind them. There is here a cruel dilemma before us. If we promoted justice and charity among men, we should be playing directly into the Enemy's hands; but if we guide them to the opposite behaviour, this sooner or later produces (for He permits it to produce) a war or a revolution, and the undisguisable issue of cowardice or courage awakes thousands of men from moral stupor.

This, indeed, is probably one of the Enemy's motives for creating a dangerous world—a world in which moral issues really come to the point. <u>He sees as well as you do that courage is not simply *one* of the virtues, but the form of every virtue at the testing point, which means, at the point of highest reality.</u> A chastity or honesty, or mercy, which yields to danger will be chaste or honest or merciful only on conditions. Pilate was merciful till it became risky.

It is therefore possible to lose as much as we gain by making your man a coward; he may learn too much about himself!

**FIELD NOTE**

## Real vs. Fantasy

Probably the scenes he is now witnessing will not provide material for an *intellectual* attack on his faith—your previous failures have put that out of your power. <u>But there is a sort of attack on the emotions which can still be tried.</u> <u>It turns on making him *feel,* when first he sees</u> <u>human remains plastered on a wall, that this is</u> <u>'what the world is *really* like' and that all his</u> <u>religion has been a fantasy.</u> You will notice that we have got them completely fogged about the meaning of the word 'real'. They tell each other, of some great spiritual experience, 'All that *really* happened was that you heard some music in a lighted building'; here 'real' means the bare physical facts, separated from the other elements in the experience they actually had. On the other hand, they will also say 'It's all very well discussing that high dive as you sit here in an armchair, but wait till you get up there and

see what it's *really* like': here 'real' is being used
in the opposite sense to mean, not the physical
facts (which they know already while discussing
the matter in armchairs) but the emotional effect those facts will have on a human consciousness. Either application of the word could be
defended; but our business is to keep the two
going at once so that the emotional value of the
word 'real' can be placed now on one side of
the account, now on the other, as it happens to
suit us. The general rule which we have now
pretty well established among them is that in all
experiences which can make them happier or
better only the physical facts are 'real' while the
spiritual elements are 'subjective'; in all experiences which can discourage or corrupt them the
spiritual elements are the main reality and to ignore them is to be an escapist. Thus in birth the
blood and pain are 'real', the rejoicing a mere
subjective point of view; in death, the terror and
ugliness reveal what death 'really means'. The
hatefulness of a hated person is 'real'—in hatred
you see men as they are, you are disillusioned;

but the loveliness of a loved person is merely a subjective haze concealing a 'real' core of sexual appetite or economic association. Wars and poverty are 'really' horrible; peace and plenty are mere physical facts about which men happen to have certain sentiments. The creatures are always accusing one another of wanting 'to eat the cake and have it'; but thanks to our labours they are more often in the predicament of paying for the cake and not eating it. Your patient, properly handled, will have no difficulty in regarding his emotion at the sight of human entrails as a revelation of Reality and his emotion at the sight of happy children or fair weather as mere sentiment.

## **Results Only**

You will soon find that the justice of Hell is
purely realistic, and concerned only with results.
Bring us back food, or be food yourself.

# AFTERWORD

Well, there it is. The demon Wormwood's personal field manual to temptation, deception, and seduction, lessons from the legendary Screwtape, senior devil and superior trainer of wannabe demons.

As it turns out, these choice bits of wisdom and instruction were purloined from Screwtape's entire body of tutorial correspondence, now famously known as *The Screwtape Letters,* which were published by C. S Lewis. Wormwood, apparently better entrepreneur than student, seized on the brilliant idea of publishing a sort of down-market tell-all, revealing trade secrets, internal politics, and embarrassing defeats. Bottom line: *The Screwtape Letters* dishes the most delicious details in hell and on earth and has become an extraordinary best-seller. Finding an agent for this work proved to be no problem since—as Wormwood lightly told the cable talk-show hosts—they all seem to have so little distance to fall. Of course, Wormwood and Screwtape are still arguing about proprietorship of the words and ideas, not to mention their major squabble over the royalty structure. And, of course, each has his own cadre of lawyers at hand. It has turned into a case study of demonic proportions, studied by demons-in-training even today.

But no matter. The question is, I suppose, what will *we* do? Will we be taken in by the lies, the diversions, the bait and switch? Do we in fact enjoy being deceived, seduced—playing the game, being in the know, an in-sider? Because, of course, we are never merely victims of fiendish intentions; we are also vol-unteers, active participants in the paths our lives take. The demons may tempt; but as they say, the choice is ours.

# INDEX OF
# SOURCES QUOTED

Page numbers in this index refer to C. S. Lewis, *The Screwtape Letters* (San Francisco: HarperCollins, 2001).

"Field Note: Do I show my fiendish face?,"
   *SL,* 31–32

USING POLITICAL OR SOCIAL STANCES

"The Strategy of Extremes," *SL,* 32–33
"Instructions on moving the Human's faith from pri-
   mary position to supporting role," *SL,* 34–35
"Field Note: Noise," *SL,* 119–120

RE: PEAKS AND TROUGHS

"Enemy Intelligence: The Law of Undulation,"
   *SL,* 37–38
"Enemy Intelligence: His Goals vs. Our Goals,"
   *SL,* 38–39
"How the Enemy utilizes the earthly phenomenon of
   peaks and troughs," *SL,* 39–40
"The Strategy of Exploitation: using the troughs," *SL,*
   45–46

RE: PLEASURE

"Enemy Intelligence: Pleasure," *SL,* 118–119
"How to use pleasure for our purposes," *SL,* 44–45
"Don't allow real pleasure! Ever!," *SL,* 63–65
"Root out the Human's personal pleasures—except of
   course for the real sins," *SL,* 65–66
"Field Note: On the subject of fun, jokes, flippancy,"
   *SL,* 54–56